venice
queen of the sea

82 Colour Plates

e Friars and the Grand Canal

St. Mark's Square and Riva degli Schiavoni

St. Mark's Church. The Horses

THE CITY OF VENICE

The City of Venice was founded on the islands of the Rivoalto (today's Rialto) in 810, when, as a result of unsettled conditions of life in the Lagoon, a group of men, headed by Agnello Partecipazio decided to leave Malamocco, their most important centre, and move to new islands in the heart of the lagoon. Not until then was Venice born in substance and in spirit. In point of fact, up till then the refugees from the mainland had considered their habitats in the Lagoon as merely temporary places of exile from the homes they had left during the Barbarian invasions. For a long time these people were linked to their regions of origin with the corresponding social, political and religious organizations, and the lands and wealth abandoned in haste. They had hoped to return quickly but as time went on their ties progressively loosened. The succeeding generations accepted the lagoon as their proper environment for the development of all facets of human activity, and began to create their own way of life in harmony with the environment and the advantages which gradually revealed themselves. They created on these islets independent and secure centres of power and wealth. The development of the inner lagoon was accompanied by a policy of territorial expansion, oftentimes bloody, in the mainland Veneto region, within the context of the vast and complex changes which marked the decline and fall of first the Roman Empire and then the rise and ultimate breakdown of Byzantine civilization. From the outset the Lagoon was considered a Byzantine dependency. At Ravenna, seat of the Exarchate, the prestigious and powerful Eastern Empire maintained a representative who governed in the Emperor's name. As Byzantium was far away and Ravenna often struggling to survive, the Venetians, while always calling on Byzantium for help when difficulties arose, were able to pursue an independent policy once they had become aware of their material and spiritual resources, their political skill and above all their commercial expertise. During the VIII cent. there was a slow development of a new political course in the area which for the two centuries previously had been defining itself geographically with reference to its special natural situation, and in addition as a permanent home for a population seeking its own scheme of internal organization. The successive phases of this search begin with the first attempts to guarantee survival and go on to the somewhat organic structuring of regulations for the increased numbers in the community, clear evidence of their wish to free themselves from a network of relationships and dependencies, often at cross-purposes, which had blocked any possibility of unity, vital to the new community. The Lagoon's inhabitants, nobles and common people, had organized themselves from the beginning to exploit the natural resources of the area. They built up a series of advantageous commercial relations, carefully refraining from political commitments to keep their commerce active.

Already in the VII cent. Venetian merchant ships had, by degrees, reached the shores of Africa, Rome could be reached overland or by sea routes up through the Tyrrhenian Sea, while heavy traffic developed with the Adri-

St. Mark's Square, S. Giorgio and the Lido

atic ports and riverside towns on the Italian mainland. If, at the beginning, private initiative had been a sufficient, even the determining factor in this activity, it is clear that a more complex organization was required to handle and regulate the increase in the volume of business, the number of navigational routes and shipping tonnage. Furthermore, official status was increasingly necessary in dealing with other states and nations, and more continuing support was necessary for the acquisition of new markets and the setting up of commercial bases for the facilitation of exchange. **Rivoalto.** These islands, which until that time, must have been overlooked or forgotten, if the rare mention of them in chronicles and even later documents is any indication, were the scene of the creation of a new social order which required a more homogeneous and aware political programme. Through the progressive unification of purpose and action the inhabitants at the Rialto participated in an increasingly complex, positive political and social experience. The indigenous spirit had by then gained a secure feeling of independence. The procedure by which Venice was built reveals an inherent purpose achieved concurrently with the search for the conditions to make it an accomplished fact. The city came into existence and grew with these precise goals. Policy dictated the make-up of the city, but in its turn was conditioned by the space available. This meant that even before the city itself came into being, the two most significant nuclei for later building had already been established: St. Mark's Square and the Rialto Market.

St. Mark's Square is therefore the concrete embodiment of ideals, where the concept of the state found its expression. This gives rise to a clearly organic interpretation of the fundamental problem and its development: the importance of the lagoon and its use, or rather, that ample but clearly delimited part of it, so that natural backgrounds at the crossing of the main waterways were carefully determined. The lagoon Basin became an environment for living. The importance and significance of this to the nascent city constituted the first fundamental stable point and permitted a consistent internal development. St. Mark's Square and the adjacent Basin became a single entity. It is therefore impossible to separate the development of each environment as it is impossible to divide the two elements. This

Grand Canal

sense of completeness was necessarily lost when the connections implicit in the system and the stretches of water joining island to island, island to mainland were considered as distances to cross and as areas of separation. This loss had already been felt long before the machine age, with its trains and cars. When Venetians lost their love of the sea, as a result of a complex series of factors, water was no longer a vital element but rather a nuisance, which gradually became forgotten. In the minds of many, Venice was limited to the sections above water level, a pedestrian zone. In this way the sense of its constituent interchange was lost. This had been the essence of the city's existence.

When Venice, the island city, was linked to the mainland (the Railway Bridge, 1848; Motor Causeway, 1930) it reversed its points of arrival and departure. A new era began in which every political, economic and social structure rapidly changed. This meant also the rise of different needs. The balance and organic functional quality of the city, and especially its urbanistic centre, St. Mark's Square, no longer corresponded to the new reality. To successive generations, however, it regained some importance either

Rio Foscari

as the historical evidence of a collective spirit determining its purpose and development or as an art form beyond any implication of transcendent spiritual values. The new links to the outside world were no longer with the time-honoured natural means: the sea. The traveller was no longer received in the majestic Lagoon Basin, but in an area diametrically opposed as the new locales were not planned to welcome him, as happens far too often in modern architecture. **From Piazzale Roma,** the car terminal, you reach the city centre by direct motorboat routes along the Rio Nuovo and Rio Foscari. Along this route, first flanked by modern constructions, you pass by the surviving elements of an arcaded loggia, now bricked up, from the ancient Ca' Foscolo, a casa-fondaco (house-warehouse) dating from the XI cent. At the entrance to the Grand Canal stands the spacious Palazzo Foscari, in middle XV cent. Gothic style, built as a sumptuous residence for Doge Francesco Foscari, who dominated the Venetian political scene for many years. He initiated the policy of expansion on the mainland Veneto region, which partially altered the economic development of the city. Here you emerge into the Grand Canal, the splendid waterway that runs through

Grand Canal at Railway Station

Grand Canal from the Scalzi Bridge, Palazzo Flangini, the Cupola and Campanile of S. Geremia

St. Mark's Basin and San Giorgio

the city from West to East. Along it the Venetians built their richest and finest residences.

The Grand Canal is the normal route for the visitor who arrives by train. With it you have the first impression of the city and become acquainted with one of the many and varied aspects of its urban planning and its special mode of being. Passing the Rialto, you can almost imagine the former bustle in the great commercial market there, with crowds from all nations busy buying and selling merchandise of every description; the ships and boats so jam-packed so as to nearly block the Canal, while waiting to unload and load their cargoes; the more distant eras when the little sandy islands were silent, partly submerged at high tide, whose few inhabitants were engaged in extracting the only wealth the water could offer: fish and salt; the enterprise of these same people, who, by bargaining with the mainland dwellers were able to procure the necessary materials for the solidification of the ground, for their houses and canal embankments. This spot can call to mind the constant effort and will to make this back-water the fulcrum of a powerful and rich political and social organization, as well as the skill necessary to bring into existence a rational city structure by utilizing the special geographical situation.

A new functional amenity, the busy **Tessera airport,** was added a few years ago, on the mainland, a few miles from Mestre. Venice can be reached from here by motorboat across the Lagoon. This route takes you past the island of Murano, with a centuries-long tradition of fine glass; then **S. Michele in Isola,** formerly a thriving monastery, called «Cavana de Muran», as it offered shelter to boats going from Venice to Murano. It is now the city cemetery. The church there, with its white façade and curvilinear pediment, was the first Renaissance religious building and designed by Mauro Coducci who began construction in 1469. Next to it is the Emiliani Chapel, built on a hexagonal floor plan in 1530 to designs by Guglielmo Bergamasco. The bell tower and inner side cloister are XV cent. Gothic. This route is the Northern approach to Venice. In the left distance you can see, set off by high crenellated walls, the old Arsenal, founded in the XII cent. and later enlarged with new basins and larger buildings (inside the walls) necessary for shipbuilding and manufacturing of equipment such as rope, sails,

S. Michele in Isola. The Church and the Emiliani Chapel

anchors etc. Then comes the side façade of the Hospice of the Mendicanti, which, with its school and church on Campo SS. Giovanni e Paolo forms one of the monumental groupings of the city (pag. 66). You can also see the Jesuit church, its tympanum topped by numerous statues, an XVIII cent. (1729) work by Domenico Rossi and G. B. Fattoretto. Nearby is the Casino degli Spiriti, a small free-standing edifice belonging to the noble Contarini family whose Palazzo is located on the Fondamenta. The house was renowned for its gala celebrations, its many gaming tables and as the venue for literary and other gatherings. Its name, of folk origin, refers to the loneliness of its position and the echoes the North wind created in the rooms and round the exterior.

Design of the Foundations of Rialto Bridge   St. Mark's Basin ▶

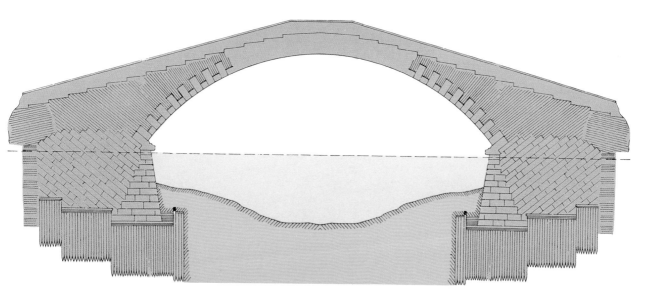

ST. MARK'S SQUARE

St. Mark's Square is certainly the best known image of Venice, a symbol identified with the city itself. In fact, when you consider each of its structures within the urban context, you can see that every one represents a significant political, social, ethical or religious entity: the Church that houses the relics of the patron saint, the Evangelist St. Mark; the Ducal Palace, seat of the Government and State authority, the Doge's Apartments, the Law Courts; the Procuratie, residences of the Procurators of St. Mark's, the State's most eminent judges; the Library housing the valuable heritage of manuscripts and incunabula; the Mint, with its economic and commercial significance; the Granary (Granai di Terranova), now no longer in existence, where the government would store reserves of foodstuffs against times of want; the Clock Tower, the Prisons, the Campanile (Bell Tower) whose bells measured out the hours of the working day, and finally, the two columns of Saints Mark and Theodore standing before the Basin, symbolically watching over the city and the lagoons.

The Square appears as a clearly planned area, backed on one side by a closely knit structural entity and open on the other to the Lagoon. The city is not made up merely of islands where the buildings stand and where you move about on foot, it is really a relationship between land that emerges from the water and the water that surrounds the land. The contact between the two elements is essential and integral. The Square is the centre of the water-land city, at the place where the two elements most clearly meet. The square is sited where various traffic lines naturally converge: The Grand Canal where it meets the vast Lagoon Basin; the Giudecca Canal, which is the shipping channel after the Lagoon is entered at St. Nicholas Inlet; and also the pedestrian route from the Rialto. In addition, the harmonious outlines of the Giudecca and San Giorgio islands give a background perspective to the waters, integrally linked with the overall unity of St. Mark's Square.

The Square has two distinct values: historical evolution and planned structural development, paralleling ideas common throughout Venetian society. The structures characterize and define the city according to its own possibilities and aspirations, so revealing its people and laws. Since the Square's purpose was clearly defined from the start, it soon became the active religious, political and social centre of the city.

The Square was brought into being down through the centuries, not only for strictly functional aims, but also in harmony with the new and changing artistic theories and ideals which reflect the constant desire to conform with and add to the canons of good taste and artistic feeling. The reconciling of function with art presupposes the presence of a special ideal and attitude which informed Venetian society and its behaviour. The first goal which remains substantially unaltered despite the passage of time was the creation of an objective world of space and mass corresponding to the needs of each period dictated by needs and policy. This response permitted the direct integration of the multiple artistic expressions and their arrangement into a coherent composition and design. St. Mark's Square displays a complete and static form; dynamically expressed in the changes undergone during its history, and proves the validity of the theory of its ideological purpose. The final expression of this artistic reality has come down to us in the pictures and descriptions that remain from previous eras, as a record of the past. An exceptional and fortunate series of events, as well as cooperation between enlightened governing officials and artists created the square, during the centuries of slow accretions, of wise acceptance of existing forms, as well as of intelligent innovation. The geometry of the space and wide, open areas as they relate to the edifices denotes the marked representative importance with which the Venetian State wanted to stress the autonomy and distinction of its city architecture.

Now it is time to consider the individual buildings, their eras and architects.

The Procuratie Vecchie (XV cent.) replaced the Byzantine edifices. Mauro Coducci's original plans provided for one floor. The old and the new buildings are similar in plan and continuity of façade. On his death Bon and Guglielmo dei Grigi erected the second level, so that it became one of the significant works of the Venetian Renaissance.

St. Mark's Square

St. Mark's Piazzetta with the Columns of Mark and Theodore.
In the background beyond the Church the Clock Tower

The Clock Tower, whose arch marks the start of one of the oldest streets
(at least as a pedestrian way) the Mercerie, leading directly from St. Mark's
to the Rialto. The central tower, another Coducci design (1496/99), has two
XVI cent. wings, probably by Pietro Lombardo. On the flat roof stands the
large bell, which marks the time by being struck by the bronze statues of
the two Moors. One of the sights of Ascension week is to see the three
Magi preceded by an angel emerging from the small door on one side,
passing across and disappearing through the other side door.

The Procuratie Nuove run along the other side of the square. In 1582, the
architect Vincenzo Scamozzi tore down the old Orseolo Hospice, adjacent
to the Campanile. (The only picture extant is in Gentile Bellini's painting
«The Procession of the Cross» in the Academy Museum.) For the new
building Scamozzi repeated the Renaissance architectural motifs of the
adjoining Marciana Library, but adding another floor. He continued the building till the tenth arcade, from where it was completed by Baldassare Longhena in 1640. The building is divided into nine apartments designed for
the Procurators of St. Mark's. At the far end of the Square is the neo-clas-
sical Napoleonic Wing by Giuseppe Soli. After the demolition of the Church

of San Geminiano in 1807, designed by Sansovino, Napoleon proposed a great ballroom to be built next to the Procuratie. Fortunately, the scheme finally decided upon caused the least damage to the overall architectural unity of the Square.

The Campanile (Bell Tower) free standing at the junction of the Piazza and the Piazzetta, acts as a dynamic fulcrum for the two inter-communicating open areas. It was first constructed as a defence and watch-tower under Doge Pietro Tribuno, at the end of IX cent. It was frequently constructed thereafter between the XII and XIV cents., raised with the addition of a belfry. By the beginning of the XVI cent., the tower had assumed its final shape. On the 14th July, 1902, the tower collapsed without warning. By 1912 it was rebuilt in the form you can see today. Its largest bell, the Marangona (from marangoni, Venetian for «carpenter») sounded when master crafts-men began and ended their labours.

At the base stands **the Loggetta,** constructed by Sansovino between 1537 and 1549. This was used as a guardhouse by the Arsenalotti (Arsenal workers) during the Great Council meetings.

In 1532 the Republic commissioned Jacopo Sansovino to design a building

St. Mark's Square

The Clock Tower
Clock Tower. The Moors ▶

Riva degli Schiavoni. In the background the Gardens   St. Mark's Church. The Façade ▶

which would worthily house the valuable codices and manuscripts bequeathed to the republic by Petrarch and Cardinal Bessarion in 1468. In 1554, its construction, beginning from the Campanile end, was constructed up to the sixteenth arcade. On Sansovino's death work stopped, but resumed under Vincenzo Scamozzi who completed it between 1583 and 1588, rounding the corner as far as the Mint, another XVI cent. building by Sansovino. Finally, on the other side of the Piazzetta and over the rio (small canal) linked to the complex of the Square's buildings by the **Bridge of Sighs,** stand the Prisons. The section facing the Basin, by Antonio da Ponte, is made almost entirely of blocks of Istrian stone. In the large rooms on the second floor above the portico were the courtrooms of the «Signori di notte al Criminal» who had a double function: preventing crime by supervision and punishing crime after due trial.

The Square's original XII cent. brick paving, laid in herring-bone pattern was replaced in 1723 by Andrea Tirali with something much more formal and orderly. The grey stone from the Euganean Hills contrasts elegantly with the white inlay. However, this caused the Square to lose its sense of intimacy, as well as the atmosphere created by the red-brown brick.

ST. MARK'S BASILICA

St. Mark's Basilica. In the beginning Venice's patron was St. Theodore, who perhaps recalled too much her dependency on Byzantium. According to an old tradition St. Mark the Evangelist came to some of the islands of the Lagoon during his journeys. When two merchants, Tribuno di Malamocco and Rustico di Torcello arrived in Venice with the Evangelist's relics, the Republic adopted him as patron saint. His symbol, the Winged Lion, became the symbol of Venice itself. With political skill the Greek saint was replaced by a Latin one to affirm an independence of spirit which reflected their political independence. This was the beginning of a national or

the centre of civic life. The Patriarch of Grado, following the constant interference of the Patriarch of Aquileia, and the decline of his region, chose to keep his residence definitively in Venice at the end of the XI century. There were as a result many disputes between the Patriarch of Grado and the Bishop of Castello because of the loose definition of the rights of each. Such disputes became at times so bitter that, at the request of the Republic itself, Pope Nicolas V, with a Bull dated 1451, joined the two offices and all the rights appertaining to the Patriarch went to the Bishop, who became Patriarch of Venice. He retained, however, his episcopal see in the church of Saint Peter's in Castello. Only in the middle of the XIX century, when the Republic had fallen, did the Bishop transfer to the church of Saint Mark's. This had ceased to be

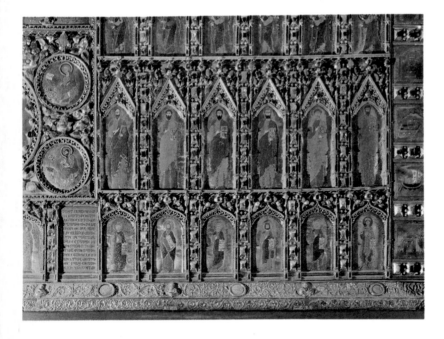

St. Mark's Church, Pala d'Oro.
Apostles and Prophets

St. Mark's Church, Narthex.
Exit from the Ark (Mosaic) ▶

State church. In fact, the ecclesiastical institution of St. Mark's had its own special structure, with a Primicerius named by the Doge, and supervised by the Procurators of St. Mark's, the highest civil officers after the Doge. The Church of St. Mark's, is by definition, the Palatine Chapel. The Basilica of St. Mark's was not only the expression of a renewed religious fervour, but also and chiefly

the ducal chapel and became, as a consequence, the episcopal see of the city.

The present Patriarchal Palace is on the site of the former where residences of the canons and the Primicerius were. Like the Ducal Palace, the church too underwent extensive changes in the first centuries of Venice's history. Reconstructions made under Doges Giovanni Partecipazio (829—836), Pietro Orse-

ETITELLEXNOEXCESSASĒTRŌ DILVVII
MARCVINNVBIB: ETERITSIGNVFEDERIS
TRŌSITVLRA
AQVE
OLLVI

St. Mark's Church, Right Nave. Floor
(Mosaic; XII cent.)

St. Mark's Church. Baptistery ▶

olo (976—978) and Domenico Contarini (1043—1071), have already been
noted. This last reconstruction gave the appearance we still see today.
Subsequent modifications were confined to decorative aspects, which,
although important and extensive, did not alter the structure. The floor
plan is a Greek Cross. The atrium or narthex surrounds the three sides of
the base of the cross internally. The pilasters of the nave support the five
large dome-shaped cupolas, covered outside by a second independent lead
one, and surmounted by an Eastern-style lantern. Outside, the façade of the
church rises in two sections. The lower has five large doorways set in
deep niches. Between the two levels is a terrace, at whose centre are the
Four Bronze Horses brought from Byzantium after the capture of the city
in the Fourth Crusade. In the shallow vault over the first doorway (left)
remains the only original mosaic, a unique depiction of the church before
the construction of the upper arcades which continued until XV cent. These
included the marble sheathing, elaborate foliage ornamentation of the
crown, the cuspids and pinnacles on the upper arcades, and the lead covered cupolas. On the large central doorway, on the inner and the outer
facings of the arch, you find a very interesting sculpture series that, inspired

St. Mark's Church, Pala d'Oro. ▶
Daniel and Salomon

St. Mark's Church, Baptistery.
Salomè's Dance

in form and subject matter by XIII cent. Romanesque plasticity, ultimately arrives at the clearly Gothic floreal and figurative style of the first half of the XIV cent. with animals in conflict, hunting scenes, the months of the year, Zodiacal signs, symbolic figures of virtue, Venetian crafts, the Prophets, and the like. As you go inside, the narthex can be seen to be lighted by round arches alternated with small, blind cuspids. The pattern of the marble mosaic pavement is the original. The vaulting is completely covered with mosaics, executed at the beginning of the XIII century. They illustrate the story of the Creation, of Cain and Abel, Abraham, Joseph, Moses, the construction of the Tower of Babel, etc. Through the large central apse-like doorway you enter the true interior of the Basilica; a deeply moving experience. Most striking is the deeply felt sense of ancient religious feeling conveyed by surroundings where the massive structure and the elaborate wall surfaces absorb and balance in a rare harmony the filtered light. Venetians' love for their church and the workmen's skill combined to enable Venice once again to possess a social and artistic masterpiece created from the XI to XV cents. The purity of the original space values, the Romanesque-Gothic additions, the capitals, columns,

St. Mark's Church, Sacristy. Ceiling Mosaic   St. Mark's Church. Interior ▶

balustrades, rare marbles, laboriously transported from the Orient and placed in this new setting, the large wall surfaces, and the gold backgrounds create surrealistic almost magical vibrations, as well as the sense of light, are all artistic manifestations of religion, but more, they are those of the social and political spirit of a people which, in different gradations, every individual participated actively. The presbytery is divided by the nave through an iconostasis, Gothic in origin, that carries the architrave above with the statues of the Virgin, St. John the Evangelist, and the Twelve Apostles, by Delle Masegne (1394). Behind the high altar is the **Pala d'Oro,** rectangular in form, an example of goldsmith's art of inestimable value, where figures of saints and virgins animate the splendid surface, enriched by pieces of enamel, gems and studded gold. The pala is the result of goldsmith craftsmanship created over a long period of time and finally completed only in the XIV century. The wall decorations were begun under Doge Domenico Selvo (1071—1084). Of this original work a few fragments still remain. The decoration was continued and developed in the XII and XIII cents. while some walls were restored even later. The mosaics cover an area of 4500 square metres.

Ducal Palace ▶

THE DOGE'S PALACE

The Doge's Palace was originally constructed in Venice from c. 800—820. Neither the existing structure, called the Olivolo Castle, the surviving defensive unit built for the new city on its inner limit facing the sea, nor the commercial buildings of the Rialto was used. The reasons for this choice of an entirely new construction are illustrated in the first chapter. An idealized reconstruction now of this first palace, housing the then government must be based on a few later documents that reproduced an earlier chronicle's description. It and public apartments of the Doge, key personality in the representation of the new state, but able to act within limits that were constantly narrowed by the power of the collective group; the government or community offices, where Venetian politics were discussed and decided in general assembly, the Palace of Justice, where the officials charged with this function were located, with court rooms and penal sections; the stables, later abolished; the living quarters for palace personnel and the palace guard; the armoury,

Map of St. Mark's

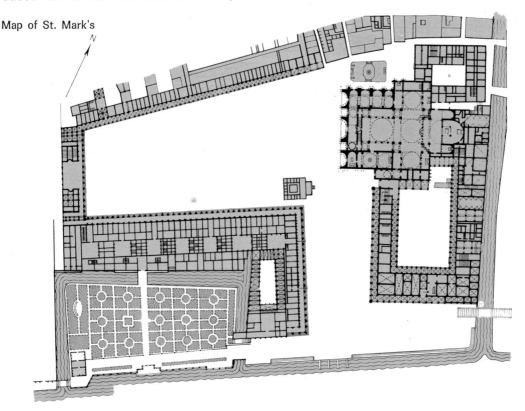

must have been defensive and in this aspect alone like a square Medieval castle. It had a surrounding wall with strong towers at its corners on the Basin side and a fortified entrance way. Inside this area, probably attached to the wall itself, were housed the State bodies. The fragmented nature of the interior and the unified continuity of the exterior suggest perhaps an internal arrangement of the sections that were subdivided according to their uses and a unified external enclosure provided by the architectural structure. In the Palace were located: the private controlled by the Council of Ten.

With Venice's growth in power and inner stability, the city, the square, and likewise the Ducal Palace began to have a different meaning and a larger psychological dimension. In the reign of Doge Sebastiano Ziani (1172—1178) a first manifest indication of this came, a sure index of an internal and external security that had been acquired. The edifices lost

St. Mark's Church, Piazzetta side. ▶
The Tetrarchs ▶

their defensive appearance, especially the Ducal Palace, opening in a new way with loggias. These are characteristic of the Byzantine period in art history. This loggia form was destined to remain even during successive epochs with all their changes. The building at the time of Doge Ziani was certainly larger than the earlier one that faced the Basin. This is where Venetian officials gathered for the Great Council in the Sala del Piovego. Only at the end of the XIII cent. did the prospect of radical reconstruction become necessary as well as an enlargement of the edifice. The work started towards the middle of the XV cent. with the renewal of the wing facing the Basin. At the entrance on the ground-level a full loggia was created. This supported the large mass of the Great Council Chamber. In 1424, under Doge Francesco Foscari, construction began on that section on the Piazzetta, continuing to the Porta della Carta. This latter was erected between 1438 and 1443 by Giovanni and Bartolomeo Bon, in florid Gothic style. When you enter this Porta della Carta, you pass through the Foscari Arch and find yourself in front of the Scala dei Giganti, by Antonio Rizzo who also planned the reconstruction of the canal side wing after the fire of 1483. The Gothic era, peculiarly so in Venetian architecture, was by then

◀Ducal Palace. Porta della Carta   Ducal Palace. Courtyard

Ducal Palace. Golden Stairway

Ducal Palace, Golden
Stairway. Stuccoes

Ducal Palace, Golden
Stairway. Stuccoes

definitely over and the Renaissance had imposed its new artistic rules. Rizzo's work was continued first by the Lombardi and then by Scarpagnino. During the reign of Doge Andrea Gritti (1523—1539), Sansovino inserted the ornate **Golden Stairway** (Scala d'Oro) in the existing structure. This became the principal way from the Loggia up to the two main upper floors and to the Apartments. Sansovino had collaborators: Tiziano Aspetti for the marble sculpture groups of the entrance portal, Alessandro Vittoria the plaster work of the vaulting, and Battista Franco the panel frescoes. The architectural outlines and masses of the palace are results of a long process of renovation and change that lasted until the XVII cent. The two main sources of inspiration, despite the length of time, have a marvellously unified design. Discontinuity appears more evidently inside where the changes of the figurative spirit differ profoundly. Venetian politics and culture were influenced by the desire to create a unified architectural entity which reflected its internal functioning. This conception resolves the problem of the function of a public building in providing for its most varied demands as well as managing to evolve it so that no single element at the highest official level would have absolute dominance over another or the others. At the same time, this was done to identify leaders and common people as clearly as possible.

Toward the end of the XVI century, two disastrous fires completely de-

Ducal Palace, Antecollege.
J. Tintoretto: Mercury and the Graces

Ducal Palace, Antecollege.
J. Tintoretto: Pallas sends away Mars

stroyed the interior of the most important halls of the palace, weakening even the walls. In 1574, fire broke out in the canal side section: the rooms of the Four Doors, of the College, and the Senate Chamber were rapidly restored afterwards. The interior decor such as the design of the ceilings and the fireplaces, the furnishings and the themes of the paintings along the walls and the panels of the ceilings was executed by Andrea Palladio, Vincenzo Scamozzi, Giovan Antonio Rusconi and Cristoforo Sorte under direction of the Palace Overseers Rusconi and then Da Ponte. The most famous painters of the time were commissioned. The most important were: Tintoretto (paintings on the ceiling of the room of the Four Doors), Titian («Doge Grimani adoring Faith»), Vicentino («The Arrival of Henry III of France at Venice»), Aliense, Jacopo Palma the Younger, and Veronese. This last was the creator of the pictures on the ceiling of the room of the College and of the canvas placed over the throne («Sebastiano Venier after the Battle of Lepanto»). The other paintings on the walls which depict Doge Alvise Mocenigo, Nicolò da Ponte, Francesco Donà and Andrea Gritti are all the work of Tintoretto.

A special note should be made on the paintings in the room of the **Antecollege:** six canvases, outstanding for their pleasant composition and rich colour. They were placed here at the beginning of the XVIII cent. substituting the original gilt leather decoration. These leather decorations were examples

Ducal Palace, Antecollege.
J. Tintoretto: Ariadne's Discovery

Ducal Palace, Antecollege.
J. Tintoretto: Vulcan's Forge

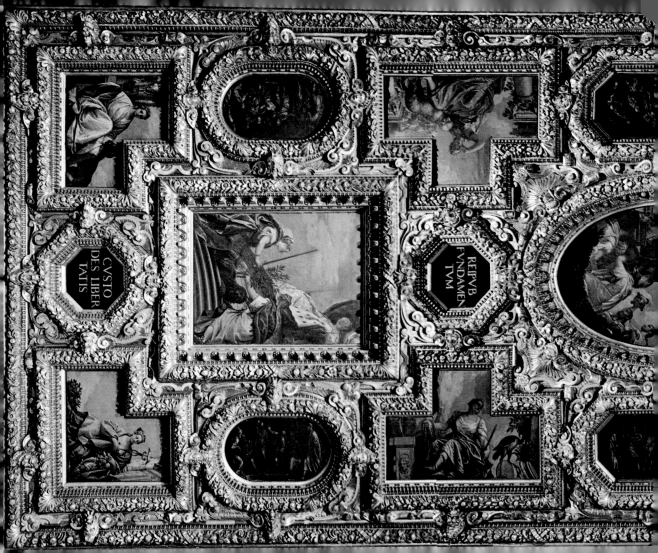

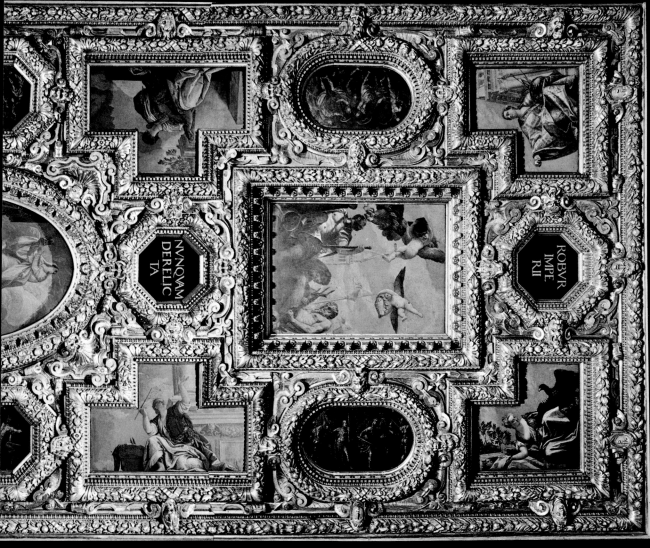

NVNQVAM DERELIC TA

ROBVR IMPE RII

of a richly artistic Venetian craftsmanship of which unfortunately only a few examples are still preserved. On the walls of the two doors are the four canvases of Tintoretto, works of the artist's mature period: **«Vulcan's Forge»**, **«Mercury and the Graces»**, **«Pallas Sends Away Mars»**, **«Ariadne's Discovery»**. On the wall across from the windows, left, are «The Rape of Europe» by Veronese, and, right, «Jacob's Return to Canaan» by Jacopo Bassano.

The second great fire, fortunately the last, broke out during the night of December 20, 1577. The fire, fanned by the wind, spread rapidly. It began from a fireplace near the Porta della Carta and only with great difficulty was it extinguished when it had reached the corner at the Ponte della Paglia. The walls as well as the stone architectural elements of the two large rooms of the Scrutiny, of the Great Council were seriously damaged. In addition the wooden sections were completely destroyed, from the roof to the floor, along with the paintings, wall frescoes and the furniture. It was a grave loss for the artistic and pictorial patrimony of Venice. Works by Gentile da Fabriano, Pisanello, Giovanni Bellini, Alvise Vivarini, Carpaccio, Titian, Paolo Veronese, and Tintoretto were all, in fact, destroyed. Of the

◀Ducal Palace, College. Ceiling   Ducal Palace. The Senate Chamber

Ducal Palace, Great Council.
F. Bassano: Presentation of
the sword to the Doge

Ducal Palace. Hall of the
Great Council

XIV cent. series only the large fresco of Guariento was saved, which can be seen in a nearby room after its detachment from its original site. The refurbishing of the Great Council Chamber and the Hall of the Scrutiny was rapidly done under Doge Nicolò da Ponte. The new pictorial series was no longer frescoed, but was done on canvas. Some of the former themes were changed, others were repeated, especially those on the ceiling, and laid out by the monk Girolamo de' Bardi and the historian Francesco Sansovino.

The Great Council was the supreme court and in it was represented the majority of the Venetian nobility. The chamber where it met was one of the largest in all Europe, measuring 54 metres in length, 25 in width, and 12 in height. The proportions and the decorations of this large room represent an imposing demonstration of the grandeur and wealth of Venice. The haste to put this room to rights worked to the detriment of its quality and as the greatest exponents of local painting, Veronese and Tintoretto, were already in advanced old age, Mannerist painters were commissioned. Mention can be made of the ceiling with canvases by Tintoretto, Veronese, Francesco da Ponte, Jacopo Palma the Younger. These were commemorative paintings of events and battles. On the walls above the throne is the large

Ducal Palace, Great Council. J. Tintoretto: Paradise

Ducal Palace, Hall Quarantia Criminal.
A. Rizzo: Eve

painting by Jacopo Tintoretto «The Coronation of the Virgin» (1590) in which hundreds of human figures are shown in ranks arranged according to the various levels of beatification. On the walls are two historic scenes, on the right is shown the historic struggle between Frederick I and Alexander III with Venice depicted in the role of mediatrix. On the left, the history of the Fourth Crusade (1201—1204) and the capture of Constantinople with the figure of Doge Enrico Dandolo. The Hall of the Scrutiny was also restored at the same period. On the left wall is the famous «Battle of Lepanto», by Andrea Vicentino. On the rear wall is the triumphal arch built in 1694 to honour Francesco Morosini, the final victor over the Turks in Morea and Peloponesia.

The construction of **the prison,** over the Rio Canonica, took fifty years after it was started in 1566. The link with the Ducal Palace was made with the noted **Bridge of Sighs** projected and built by Antonio Contin at the beginning of the XVII century. Through two parallel passageways, prisoners were led from their cells to the courtrooms and vice versa, for questioning and for sentencing. The name «of Sighs» is the result of Romantic literature, especially critical of Venetian institutions generally.

◀ Ducal Palace. Piazzetta Façade   Bridge of Sighs

THE GRAND CANAL

The Grand Canal (called Canal Grande or also Canalazzo) is the largest waterway that crosses the city. It divides the city into two large sections, with three of the city's six zones on each side. Leaving Saint Mark's Square, the canal reaches a point near Ca' Foscari then Rialto and finally Santa Chiara (Piazzale Roma) after making two large bends. This is the extreme western boundry of Venice itself. The distance is about four kilometres and the width varies from thirty to sixty metres. It is most probable that the canal was originally a branch of a river when rivers emptied directly into the lagoon. Perhaps it formed Rio Businacus that passed by Rialto where, in the first years, Venetian commercial life was busiest, before the city itself had been founded. On its banks the first fondaco (house-warehouse) was built by the merchants. The

one at the Accademia (1932), one at the Railway Station, of stone, with a single arch, the work of Miozzi, replacing one in iron that had dated from the middle of the XIX cent., built in the time of the Austrian occupation of Venice, and finally, Rialto Bridge, where a bridge had existed from the earliest days, first made of boats and then of wood set on pilings as a draw-bridge at its centre. After much discussion and the commissioning of various projects, among which the best known is Palladio's, it was only in 1588 that the construction of a stone bridge was decided. Antonio da Ponte made the plans with his nephew Antonio Contin. In 1591 the bridge, even to its upper surface where shops were planned, had been completed. At several points along the canal the two sides are linked by «Traghetti» (ferries) of gondolas that carry people back and forth. The edifices almost all rise directly from the water's edge. Only in a few places is the canal edge in the form of a fondamenta.

Grand Canal at Ca' Foscari

Grand Canal at Rialto

boats and ships came there to unload the most varied of cargoes into the storerooms of the ground floors. During the centuries the houses of the richest families were built along this principal water course. They replaced the smaller and by then ruinous structures of the preceding centuries. At present the Grand Canal is crossed by three bridges: a wooden

Now follow the route of the Grand Canal, starting from Saint Mark's Square, and observe its most important edifices. (At the left) After the Custom House (Dogana da Mar) and the Episcopal Seminary, stands **the church of Santa Maria della Salute.** On October 22, 1630, the Venetian government, in thanks for the cessation of a very serious plague, de-

Grand Canal. Church of the Salute

cided to erect this large votive temple. The plans selected were those of Baldassare Longhena, who started work on the construction immediately (1631 to 1681), on the site of the ancient Trinity Hospice. The structure, in addition to demonstrating in itself architectural and planimetric resolutions of the demands of the task, took on an exceptional significance in the overall planning for the city and the immediate surroundings at the entry to the Grand Canal. Undoubtedly, the work is not only Longhena's most important work, but also the most important of the XVII cent. in Venice. (At the right) The vast Palazzo Corner della Ca' Grande was built by command of Jacopo Corner between 1532 and 1561 to plans by Jacopo Sansovino. Just after the Academy Bridge (on the left) is the complex of buildings that formed the original Charity Monastery that has now been partially pulled down and transformed. The Scuola (school) and cloisters now house **the Academy Art Gallery,** the finest in the city, with works dating from Venice's origin to XVIII cent. Painters represented include Paolo Veneziano, the Vivarini, Jacobello del Fiore, the Bellini, Vittore Carpaccio, Giorgione, Tintoretto, Veronese, Bassano, Tiepolo, etc.

(On the right) Across from the Campo dell'Accademia lies the Palazzo

Giustinian-Lolin, one of Longhena's first Venetian works that reformed a previously existing Gothic building. Maintenance of the earlier structure forced certain architectural inharmonious results, like the very lengthened form of the windows. On the left side, the Gothic **Palazzo Loredan,** called «of the Ambassador» because it was in the XVIII cent. the site of the Roman Embassy to the Republic. The architectural characteristics show that it dates from the end of the XV cent. with its typical grouped windows enhanced with quatrefoils.

Farther on, after **Rio San Barnaba,** stands Ca' Rezzonico. In 1667, the Bon family gave Longhena the task of planning and building the edifice. The construction, halted when the first floor had been completed on the death of the artist, was only taken up again in 1750 by Giorgio Massari after the palace had passed to the Rezzonico family. The architect built the second floor to Longhena's plans and added at the rear of the building a very large ballroom. This palace now houses the museum of the Venetian XVIII cent. where are exhibited paintings and furniture in surroundings reconstructed according to the fashions of that time. A little farther on, stand the Gothic structures of Palazzo Giustinian and Palazzo Foscari, exceptional for their

Grand Canal. S. Vidal

purity of line. The group of the three buildings occupies a stretch that ends at the corner of Rio Foscari. The construction dates from the middle of the XV cent. and is possibly the work of the family of architects and sculptors Giovanni and Bartolomeo Bon, who were the most active builders of that period. The two Giustinian palaces display a unified façade that hides in a certain sense two separate units clearly divided by a street.

On the other side of Rio Foscari stands **Palazzo Balbi,** built between 1582 and 1590, perhaps by Alessandro Vittoria. The architectural elements of the façade show how the classic XVI cent. fashion was evolving toward the greater liberty and plasticity that foretold the coming of the Baroque. (On the right) After Campo San Samuele can be seen first Palazzo Grassi, by the architect Giorgio Massari (1748—1776), and then Palazzo Morolin, that is the product of a restructuring of two adjacent Gothic edifices. The plans are attributed to Sebastiano Mazzoni. The Mocenigo Palazzi have their origin in a series of XIV cent. Gothic edifices the family owned here. Around 1580, the construction of the first palace was started, called Casa Nuova, where Sansovino's and Palladio's Renaissance designs began to change to new architectural forms. The last palace built, called «Casa Vecchia», was

◀ Rio S. Barnaba

Grand Canal. Palazzo Contarini »dagli Scrigni» and Palazzo Loredan dell'Ambasciatore

Grand Canal. Ca' Foscari with Rio and Palazzo Balbi

rebuilt internally and had a completely new façade added about the XVII century. These two buildings were later joined by two identical ones to form a single front. It was here in 1592 that Giordano Bruno lived, and was informed on by his host to the Inquisition, as well as Ann, Countess of Shrewsbury, in 1621, whose relations with the Patrician Antonio Foscarini was the cause for his being charged with treason against the state and condemned to death. Near the vaporetto (waterbus) dock of S. Tomà, but very far back from the Grand Canal, stands the house in Gothic style in which the Venetian playwright Carlo Goldoni was born in 1707 and where he lived. Concerning this artist it will be noted here only that his plays, in addition to their intrinsic artistic merit, display a full and inexhaustible annotation of the life of his times, in customs and habits, and generally all the Venetian social structure. Theatre was one of the great passions of the Venetians. Venice had at one time a great number of theatres, both public and private, most of which are now vanished. Crowds gaily flocked to every performance. Poor Goldoni was forced by the number of requests that came from the constant success he had to work hard to keep up with

Rio S. Tomà

his contracts by writing one play after another. These renewed the theatre stylistically and scenically among their other merits.

When you disembark and go a little distance away from the Grand Canal, you enter the picturesque **Campo S. Tomà.** Before you, on the two short sides, stand the church of the same name and the Scuola dei Calegheri (Shoemakers) built in the second half of the XV century. Visible from here is the bell tower of Santa Maria dei Frari, one of the most important religious structures in the city. It, together with the church of SS. Giovanni e Paolo, is a good example of the form that Gothic architecture took on in Venice between XIV and XV centuries. Begun at the apse end in 1340, it could be considered as finished only in 1443 and was not consecrated until 1469. The interior is of impressive grandeur, with three naves divided by powerful columns that support a high ceiling in the form of a pointed arch cross vault. In the centre nave, before the transept, according to the liturgical rites of the times, is still found the Monks' Choir, a very rare example on account of the changes that these structures underwent in later centuries. The rare wooden choir stalls done in three series are the work of Marco Cozzi in 1468. Along the walls of the church important funerary monuments exemplify the transformation from the Gothic style to the Renaissance. The centre chapel houses Titian's masterpiece: **«The Assumption»** (1518). In the sacristy is Giovanni Bellini's «Virgin with Cherubs and Angelic Musicians» (1488). Other very important works include: Vivarini's polyptych (1482), Donatello's painted wooden sculpture depicting St. John the Baptist, and Titian's «Pesaro Panel».

(At the left) By now the **Rialto Bridge** is in view and you find Palazzo Coccina-Tiepolo, dating from the middle of the XVI cent., which is the work of Guglielmo dei Grigi, and then following it a series of Byzantine edifices that are partly reconstructed and altered. The Barzizza, Businello, and Donà Palaces recall the building activity and styles of the XII and XIII cents., in a zone that was then heavily populated owing to the economic activity of the nearby Rialto Market.

(In front, to the right) The Loredan-Corner and Dandolo-Farsetti Palaces, both from the XII cent., utilize in a stately manner the traditional Byzantine fondaco motifs with a central portico on the ground level and a full loggia on the second floor. During the XVI cent., two additional floors were added.

Friars' Church. Titian: The Assumption

Friars' Church. Titian: Pesaro Altarpiece (Detail)

Campo S. Tomà

Friars' Church ▶

The buildings are now the offices of the city government. Going under the Rialto Bridge you see on the left the present market with a long structure with arcades that was constructed by Antonio Scarpagnino after the severe fire of 1514 that destroyed the entire zone. An important state finance office is located in Palazzo dei Camerlenghi, built to plans by Antonio dei Grigi between 1525 and 1528. This is an important example of Renaissance architecture in Venice. Across the canal stands the Fondaco dei Tedeschi, constructed and leased to the foreign community in the Republic so that its merchants could conduct their commercial affairs there. It served both as a storehouse and a hotel. Giorgio Spavento and Scarpagnino designed it in 1508. At one time the façade was frescoed by Giorgione. A little farther on (on the right) stands another dwelling-storehouse, Ca' da Mosto, dating from the XII century. This too was modified by the addition of two upper floors. From here came the celebrated Venetian navigators and explorers of the same name. From 1500 throughout the 1700's the building was the «White Lion Hotel», the most noted and luxurious in the city. Here stayed, among others, Emperor Joseph II and the Counts del Nord. At the beginning of XV cent., on a site previously owned by the Zen, Marino Contarini

Friars' Church. Donatello: St. John the Baptist

Rio del Lovo

Rialto Bridge

had the **Ca' d'Oro** built. It was given this name as a result of the brilliance of its gilding and the many colours of its façade, as well as for the richness of its architecture. The structure was completed in 1434. At first the architect was Matteo Raverti, aided by the Lombardo craftsmen. Later these were replaced by the brothers Giovanni and Bartolomeo Bon. While the structural elements of the portico recall those of the Byzantine palaces, the architectural resolutions of the two loggias and the side single lancets represent the most elaborate expression of florid Gothic style, in which marble was cut into tracery and interlaced shapes. In the interior courtyard, a staircase, the work of Raverti, at one time roofed, leads to the great hall on the main floor.

(On the left) Continuing the journey along the canal, you see **Palazzo Corner della Regina.** In 1724, the architect Domenico Rossi started construction on the site of the previous Corner palazzo, belonging to the branch of the family called «of the Queen» as it was descended directly from Catherine, Queen of Cyprus, born in 1454. The edifice, set apart between two streets, has a very narrow façade in which are seen the mixture of XVII cent. architectural details with those of a fashion that had become by then neo-

Ca' d'Oro

Palazzo Corner della Regina and Palazzo Pesaro

classical. Just a little farther on you come to the most monumental palace in the city: **Ca' Pesaro.** The wealthy Pesaro family commissioned in 1652 Baldassare Longhena to draw the plans for the edifice. When, in 1658, Giovanni Pesaro was elected Doge, work had already been started on the interior section on the ground level of the courtyard. Work then went on towards the canal front until, in 1679, the façade had been finished up to the first floor level. Three years later both Longhena and Leonardo Pesaro died, so construction was halted. Later, the building was further worked on by Antonio Gaspari, who brought to an end the work on the façade by constructing it to the level of the third floor to the plans of Longhena. He also completed the rear sections around the courtyard, unified it by giving it an original kind of architectural exterior, the part on the Due Torri Canal. He built along the curved line of the canal's natural outline. About 1700, the palace was completed. Today the Gallery of Modern Art is located here, with a fine collection of paintings and sculpture (XIX/XX cents.).

(On the left) After Ca' Pesaro you will see: the Campo and the Church of San Stae, the latter reconstructed in 1678 by Giovanni Grassi and completed with a new façade by Domenico Rossi in 1709. The Belloni-Battagia

Palace by Baldassare Longhena, the Fondaco del Megio, built by the Republic in the XV cent. as a public granary, the Fondaco dei Turchi. This structure was erected in the first half of the XIII cent. for Giacomo Palmieri and later acquired by the Republic which offered it as a temporary residence to the Marquis of Ferrara, the Emperor of Byzantium, Giovanni Paleologo, to Alfonso d'Este and to others. Finally, it was leased to the Turkish community and in this way became the living quarters for their merchants and the warehouse for goods coming from the Orient. The state of the building in the XIX cent. was so poor that a radical restoration of it was made, unfortunately, however, a complete rebuilding was done and it was falsified as to original form and significance. In this same stretch of canal on the right Palazzo Vendramin-Calergi makes itself felt as a result of its mass and the purity of its lines. This work of the architect Mauro Coducci is one of the most important examples of Venetian Renaissance architecture. To be especially noted is the use, unique to the artist, of the double lancet windows that are joined under a single arch. On Canale di Cannaregio, set back a little, stands the monumental Palazzo Labia, a construction dating from the middle of the XVIII cent. by the architect Alessandro Tremignon.

Rio Pesaro

Rio dei Mendicanti and the School of St. Mark's

When the Canal reaches the railway station, you see two churches, almost facing each other, St. Mary of Nazareth (the Discalced Carmelites) and St. Simon the Less. The former was begun in 1660 to plans by Longhena, completed in 1680 with Giuseppe Sardi's façade. The latter is the work of Giovanni Scalfarotto who constructed it between the years 1718 and 1738. It is characterized by a large green dome similar to that of the Salute church. A little farther on the course of the Grand Canal is at an end.

In the Castello zone, toward the northern edge of the lagoon, an important monumental centre exists that gathers around the **Campo of SS. Giovanni e Paolo,** with the church of the same name, the large School of Saint Mark's and the Ospizio dei Mendicanti. In the centre of the campo stands the famous equestrian statue of Bartolomeo Colleoni, Mercenary, Soldier of Fortune, Captain of the Republic. The statue was erected in 1488 to a model by Andrea Verrocchio. Alessandro Leopardi directed the casting of the statue and the plans for the base on which it stands. The building of the church of SS. Giovanni e Paolo (Saints John and Paul) lasted throughout two centuries. It was consecrated in 1430. The interior has three aisles, on the plan of an Egyptian cross with five apse chapels. Here, as in the Frari church,

Campo SS. Giovanni e Paolo.
A. Verrocchio: B. Colleoni

the Gothic style is strongly marked in the architectural plan. The impressiveness is increased by the strong light that is the result of the apse's facing south. The church came right after the Basilica of Saint Mark's in order of importance in the city. The Council and the Doge came yearly to celebrate the victory of the Dardanelles here and also took part in the feast of the name day of the church itself. Doges and other important personages were buried here with full pomp and circumstance. The funeral monuments that still survive are works of importance in the history of Venetian plastic arts. Especially so are those from the Renaissance. Another important example of the art of the period at the end of the XVI cent., as much for its unity of execution as for the elegance of its line is the Chapel of the Rosary, planned and built by Alessandro Vittoria. The latter's paintings were, however, destroyed in a fire and replaced, after the rebuilding of the ceiling, with canvases by Veronese. The church has many paintings in its interior by artists such as Giovanni Bellini, Vivarini, Lorenzo Lotto, Palma, Piazzetta, and others.

Next to the church is the large **School of Saint Mark's,** started by the Lombardi in 1487, and continued after only three years by Mauro Coducci.

◄ Ca' Minelli «del Bovolo». Stairway   La Fenice Theatre

VISIT TO MURANO

The island of Murano, refuge, as were the other islands of the lagoon, for the people who had fled from the mainland pursued by the Barbarians' invasions, developed slowly. It first linked itself economically to Torcello and then to Venice. The island reached its maximum splendor when its glass industry became a byword in Europe for its quality and value. The exact date when glass making in Venice was begun is unknown. The art, handed down from the Romans, was surely brought to the lagoons by travellers, but had its decisive impetus as a result of frequent contacts with the East. Glass had been made for some time in Venice when the Republic ordered the transfer of all factories to Murano. This regulation was adopted to prevent fires, so very dangerous in that period because the houses were largely made of wood. In this way Murano acquired its special artistic and

European markets. For many centuries Venetian glass had no rivals. Its reputation declined only when the Republic itself fell. The master glass blowers were held in such high esteem that a Venetian nobleman could even marry the daughter of a master craftsman without fear of losing his own noble state. Murano itself enjoyed a certain administrative autonomy. It had its own council and the original families on the island were inscribed in a Golden Book and enjoyed special privileges. **The Glass Museum,** housed in the former residence of the Bishops of Torcello, Palazzo Giustiniani, contains more than four thousand pieces from ancient and modern times. This valuable collection documents the history and development of the Murano glass industry. The oldest surviving examples of glass are those from the middle of the XIV cent. like the goblets and glasses with surfaces that

Burano
Murano, Church of St. Mary and ▶
Donatus. Apse and Campanile

Murano Glass

economic aspect. Scores of glass furnaces were set up on the island and glass blowing became consequently the largest source for employment and income for the inhabitants who constantly increased. The quality of the production, the originality of the forms and the perfection of the techniques captured the

have deep tints of red-blue-green on which the master decorator painted in enamel to create scenes of weddings, erotic scenes, portraits of married couples, etc. «The Wedding Goblet» is famous. Only at the beginning of the XIV cent. did transparent white glass come into use. Other techniques were adopted

after its introduction: diamond engraving, gold leaf application, the making of frosted glass, milk glass, and patterns of fine net and filigree work.

If you stop momentarily before you quit this industrial island to stand before and then enter **Saint Mary and Saint Donatus,** you will see the oldest church in Venice. This church forms, taken together with the Baptistry and the government office, the chief institutional nucleus of the island. It was rebuilt of open brickwork in the first half of the XII cent. (consecrated in 1140). The floor plan is typically that of a three-nave basilica. The pavement is multi-coloured mosaic with ornamental patterns and animal figures. On the hollow of the apse is preserved the largest mosaic that is contemporaneous with the construction of the edifice. The simplicity of the front contrasts with the richness and architectural fantasy of the apse area. On the outside, this area is divided into two levels: the false portico and the open loggia along the octagonal perimeter of the central apse section. In the XIX cent. the island structures were seriously neglected. Many of the important edifices are now rapidly disappearing (fifteen churches, monasteries, hospices, academies etc.). This original community grouping, having already been so endangered, after the year 1945 suffered additional damage.

Glass Making

VISIT TO TORCELLO

Leaving behind both Venice and Murano, you can go across the lagoon lengthwise towards a group of islands of incomparable beauty: Burano, Mazzorbo, Torcello, and, a little farther removed, San Francesco del Deserto. The inexhaustible fascination of the lagoon landscape, its profound silence from ancient times, the sense of tranquil and serene solitude, the social characteristics of its inhabitants, and the architectural characteristics of the building groups make up an unforgettable image of a singularly subtly impressive open space. On these islands and on others that have now vanished, on these barren sandbanks and along the silent canals the first inhabitants came when they had escaped the ravages of war on the mainland. They were able to create and populate rich cities and to bring to life a highly profitable commerce. Torcello and its archipelago became a political and religious

Torcello. The Canal

centre of notable importance. In addition to its market, which is found mentioned in the oldest documents, houses and palaces, churches and monasteries were built, filled with memorials of the past and art treasures.

Costanziaca, peopled in the remotest times by the Altinati, was already deserted and a swamp in the XVII century. Now with all its buildings, it is completely submerged underwater. Ammiana, also filled with churches and monasteries, after its abandonment and its slow sinking, became a squalid salt-pit. The change of the physical environment, as a result of the deposits of rivers, the formation of swamps and marshy areas, the sinking of the land in a rather rapid way, all resulted in the decline and the abandonment of this group of islands. Several important religious structures remain recalling the past glories. The churches of St. Mary Genetrix and St. Fosca.

Remains of a stone tablet, dated 639, confirm the hypothesis that the first construction of the **church of St. Mary Genetrix** dates from the VII century. Toward the end of the same century, in 697, following the intensification of the migrations to the islands. the church was rebuilt and enlarged. When it became the episcopal see's cathedral, the church acquired a notable importance and prestige. In 864 another reconstruction was effected. The structure was enlarged both in length and in width, by the addition of two side aisles. The level of the presbytery was raised to make room for a crypt. The last major restoration, during which the columns and capitals of the central nave, the wooden ceiling and the marble mosaic pavement were renewed, dates from 1008. That was the time when Orso, the son of Doge Pietro II Orseolo, was elevated to the episcopal throne of Torcello. The bell tower too can be dated from the same period.

Many of the interior wall surfaces are covered with precious XII cent. mosaics, despite the iconographic similarity to those of the VII-VIII centuries. The affinity of the mosaic above the entrance door, depicting «The Last Judgment» with some of the mosaics of Saint Mark's Basilica suggests that the same craftsmen created them both or that they were of the same epoch as the Venetian-Byzantine school active in XII cent. Venice. **The church of St. Fosca,** erected perhaps first in 864, was reconstructed in the X cent. on a central Greek cross floor plan. The little portico that runs outside on five sides of the octagonal form is characteristic. The nearby museum, in the former Palazzo del Consiglio, houses marble fragments, sculpture and bas-relief sculpture of the Venetian-Byzantine school as well as tombs, sarcophagi and Roman and Early Christian funeral stele.

San Francesco del Deserto, with the impressive green of its high cypresses and little vineyards is a reminder of the original natural appearance of similar places in the lagoon area. The fame of the island is due to the visit of Saint Francis, who landed here in 1220. He remained, charmed by the peace of the surroundings and the simplicity of the life there. You come, finally, to **Burano,** the largest and most heavily populated island. In the past, it had periods of prosperity, owing above all to the lace industry, which has continued into our own day, although in a much reduced manner. In the XVII cent. its lace pattern, called «punto in aria», became famous. This stitch technique, invented in Burano, created an open-work cloth with the use of a single thread in patterns of geometric motifs, as well as animals and flowers. The island can be seen from a distance lying along the pale and flat lagoon with its own barely emerging outline. The vivacity of the

Torcello. The Square

Burano. A Canal

colours of the façades of the low, modest houses and the outline of the leaning bell tower catch the eye. The inhabitants live chiefly from fishing. The structural arrangement is largely preserved, if not by original buildings, by the type of building still standing. The canals wind around across the island and are full of boats. Fishermen while awaiting nightfall prepare their nets and the little squares are constantly alive with people. These are fragments of an older life that exists even today, examples of the intimate links that have remained across the centuries between this community and its lagoon surroundings.

◀ Torcello, Church of St. Mary Genetrix.
Apse Mosaic

Venice. Sunset ▶

INDEX

CANAL GRANDE   TERRAFERMA   PONTE DI RIALTO   TEATRO LA FENICE   MURANO   S. MICHELE   SS. GIOVANNI E PAOLO   PIAZ

CANAL GRAN